MAD LIBS®

VACATION FUN

By Roger Price and Leonard Stern

PSS!
PRICE STERN SLOAN

PRICE STERN SLOAN
Published by the Penguin Group
Penguin Group (USA) Inc., 375 Hudson Street, New York, New York 10014, USA
Penguin Group (Canada), 90 Eglinton Avenue East,
Suite 700, Toronto, Ontario M4P 2Y3, Canada
(a division of Pearson Penguin Canada Inc.)
Penguin Books Ltd., 80 Strand, London WC2R 0RL, England
Penguin Group Ireland, 25 St. Stephen's Green, Dublin 2, Ireland
(a division of Penguin Books Ltd.)
Penguin Group (Australia), 250 Camberwell Road, Camberwell,
Victoria 3124, Australia
(a division of Pearson Australia Group Pty. Ltd.)
Penguin Books India Pvt. Ltd., 11 Community Centre, Panchsheel Park,
New Delhi—110 017, India
Penguin Group (NZ), 67 Apollo Drive, Rosedale, Auckland 0632, New Zealand
(a division of Pearson New Zealand Ltd.)
Penguin Books (South Africa) (Pty.) Ltd., 24 Sturdee Avenue,
Rosebank, Johannesburg 2196, South Africa

Penguin Books Ltd., Registered Offices:
80 Strand, London WC2R 0RL, England

Published by Price Stern Sloan,
a division of Penguin Young Readers Group,
345 Hudson Street, New York, New York 10014.

ISBN 978-0-8431-1921-3

58

MAD LIBS®
INSTRUCTIONS

MAD LIBS® is a game for people who don't like games!
It can be played by one, two, three, four, or forty.

• RIDICULOUSLY SIMPLE DIRECTIONS

In this tablet you will find stories containing blank spaces where words are left out. One player, the READER, selects one of these stories. The READER does not tell anyone what the story is about. Instead, he/she asks the other players, the WRITERS, to give him/her words. These words are used to fill in the blank spaces in the story.

• TO PLAY

The READER asks each WRITER in turn to call out a word—an adjective or a noun or whatever the space calls for—and uses them to fill in the blank spaces in the story. The result is a MAD LIBS® game.

When the READER then reads the completed MAD LIBS® game to the other players, they will discover that they have written a story that is fantastic, screamingly funny, shocking, silly, crazy, or just plain dumb—depending upon which words each WRITER called out.

• EXAMPLE (*Before* and *After*)

" _____ !" he said _____
EXCLAMATION   ADVERB

as he jumped into his convertible _____ and
                                                          NOUN

drove off with his _____ wife.
                              ADJECTIVE

" _____*Ouch!*_____ !" he said _____*Stupidly*_____
EXCLAMATION   ADVERB

as he jumped into his convertible _____*Cat*_____ and
                                                          NOUN

drove off with his _____*brave*_____ wife.
                              ADJECTIVE

In case you have forgotten what adjectives, adverbs, nouns, and verbs are, here is a quick review:

An ADJECTIVE describes something or somebody. *Lumpy, soft, ugly, messy,* and *short* are adjectives.

An ADVERB tells how something is done. It modifies a verb and usually ends in "ly." *Modestly, stupidly, greedily,* and *carefully* are adverbs.

A NOUN is the name of a person, place or thing. *Sidewalk, umbrella, bridle, bathtub,* and *nose* are nouns.

A VERB is an action word. *Run, pitch, jump,* and *swim* are verbs. Put the verbs in past tense if the directions say PAST TENSE. *Ran, pitched, jumped,* and *swam* are verbs in the past tense.

When we ask for a PLACE, we mean any sort of place: a country or city *(Spain, Cleveland)* or a room *(bathroom, kitchen.)*

An EXCLAMATION or SILLY WORD is any sort of funny sound, gasp, grunt, or outcry, like *Wow!, Ouch!, Whomp!, Ick!,* and *Gadzooks!*

When we ask for specific words, like a NUMBER, a COLOR, an ANIMAL, or a PART OF THE BODY, we mean a word that is one of those things, like *seven, blue, horse,* or *head*.

When we ask for a PLURAL, it means more than one. For example, *cat* pluralized is *cats*.

MAD LIBS® is fun to play with friends, but you can also play it by yourself! To begin with, DO NOT look at the story on the page below. Fill in the blanks on this page with the words called for. Then, using the words you have selected, fill in the blank spaces in the story.

Now you've created your own hilarious MAD LIBS® game!

BEARS

ADJECTIVE_____

NOUN _____

PLURAL NOUN _____

ADJECTIVE_____

ADJECTIVE_____

VERB ENDING IN "ING" _____

VERB ENDING IN "ING" _____

ADJECTIVE_____

ADJECTIVE_____

NOUN _____

FOOD (PLURAL)_____

PART OF THE BODY (PLURAL) _____

ADJECTIVE_____

VEHICLE _____

FOOD (PLURAL)_____

FOOD (PLURAL)_____

SOMETHING ALIVE (PLURAL) _____

SOMETHING ALIVE (PLURAL) _____

ADVERB_____

NOUN _____

MAD LIBS®
BEARS

If you go to some _____ place like Yellowstone
ADJECTIVE

National _____ , you must know how to deal with the
NOUN

wild animals such as bears and wolves and _____ . The
PLURAL NOUN

most important of these is the bear. There are three kinds of bears,

the grizzly bear, the _____ bear, and the _____
ADJECTIVE   ADJECTIVE

bear. Bears spend most of their time _____ or
VERB ENDING IN "ING"

_____ . They look very_____ , but if you
VERB ENDING IN "ING"   ADJECTIVE

make them _____ , they might bite your _____ .
ADJECTIVE   NOUN

Bears will come up to your car and beg for _____ .
FOOD (PLURAL)

They will stand on their hind legs and clap their _____
PART OF THE BODY (PLURAL)

together and pretend to be _____ . But do not get out
ADJECTIVE

of your _____ or offer the bears _____ or
VEHICLE   FOOD (PLURAL)

_____ . This same advice applies to other wild creatures
FOOD (PLURAL)

such as _____ and _____ . Remem-
SOMETHING ALIVE (PLURAL)   SOMETHING ALIVE (PLURAL)

ber all these rules and you will spend your vacation _____
ADVERB

and not get eaten by a/an _____ .
NOUN

From VACATION FUN MAD LIBS® • Copyright © 1988 by Price Stern Sloan,
a division of Penguin Putnam Books for Young Readers, New York.

MAD LIBS® is fun to play with friends, but you can also play it by yourself! To begin with, DO NOT look at the story on the page below. Fill in the blanks on this page with the words called for. Then, using the words you have selected, fill in the blank spaces in the story.

Now you've created your own hilarious MAD LIBS® game!

VACATION DIALOGUE

NAME (FEMALE) _____

CELEBRITY (MALE) _____

NOUN _____

NOUN _____

NAME (MALE) _____

NOUN _____

ADJECTIVE _____

NUMBER _____

NOUN _____

VERB ENDING IN "ING" _____

CELEBRITY (FEMALE) _____

VERB ENDING IN "ING" _____

ADJECTIVE _____

VERB ENDING IN "ING" _____

ADJECTIVE _____

TYPE OF SHOE (PLURAL) _____

PLURAL NOUN _____

MAD LIBS®
VACATION DIALOGUE

GIRL: Hello. My name is ___Sally___.
NAME (FEMALE)

BOY: Hi. My name is ___Finn___. I came here with
CELEBRITY (MALE)

my mother and father and my little ___sister___.
NOUN

GIRL: I am here with my best girl ___friend___. We are
NOUN

staying at the ___Jefferson___ Hilton Hotel.
NAME (MALE)

BOY: I hear they have a great ___pool___ there. How is
NOUN

the food?

GIRL: ___good___. But the room only costs ___15___
ADJECTIVE   NUMBER

dollars a day.

BOY: I rented a/an ___pool___ for this afternoon. Maybe
NOUN

you and I could go ___swimming___.
VERB ENDING IN "ING"

GIRL: I'd love to, but I promised ___Katy Perry___ I'd go
CELEBRITY (FEMALE)

___dancing___ with her.
VERB ENDING IN "ING"

BOY: Well, tonight there is a/an ___awful___ Dance at the
ADJECTIVE

Hotel ___swining___ Room.
VERB ENDING IN "ING"

GIRL: I'd love to go to that. Is it formal?

BOY: Yes, be sure and wear a/an ___purple___ dress and your
ADJECTIVE

___high heels___. I am going to wear my ___tototo___.
TYPE OF SHOE (PLURAL)   PLURAL NOUN

MAD LIBS® is fun to play with friends, but you can also play it by yourself! To begin with, DO NOT look at the story on the page below. Fill in the blanks on this page with the words called for. Then, using the words you have selected, fill in the blank spaces in the story.

Now you've created your own hilarious MAD LIBS® game!

CAVE EXPLORING

VERB ENDING IN "ING" _____

ADJECTIVE_____

NUMBER _____

ADJECTIVE_____

PLACE _____

ADJECTIVE_____

PLURAL NOUN _____

ADJECTIVE_____

ADJECTIVE_____

COLOR_____

COLOR_____

ADJECTIVE_____

ADJECTIVE_____

ADJECTIVE_____

ADJECTIVE_____

PLURAL NOUN _____

NOUN _____

MAD LIBS®
CAVE EXPLORING

If you like to go _____ in _____
            VERB ENDING IN "ING"   ADJECTIVE

caves that are _____ feet underground, you should go to the
                NUMBER

_____ Mammoth Caves located in _____ .
     ADJECTIVE   PLACE

Thousands of _____ _____ go there
                  ADJECTIVE   PLURAL NOUN

every summer. Crawling about in caves is called "spelunking." And it

is really a/an _____ sport. But always go with a/an
                  ADJECTIVE

_____ guide so you won't get lost. Once in the cave, you
    ADJECTIVE

will see beautiful _____ and _____ rocks and
                      COLOR   COLOR

crystals. Huge _____ things hang from the ceiling and
                  ADJECTIVE

are called "stalagtites." Huge _____ things jut up from
                                    ADJECTIVE

the floor and are called "stalagmites." Caves are homes for millions of

_____ bats. Bats can fly and look like _____
    ADJECTIVE   ADJECTIVE

rats. Spelunking is dangerous, so be sure to wear special shoes with

_____ on them and a hat with a battery-powered _____ .
   PLURAL NOUN   NOUN

From VACATION FUN MAD LIBS® • Copyright © 1988 by Price Stern Sloan,
a division of Penguin Putnam Books for Young Readers, New York.

MAD LIBS® is fun to play with friends, but you can also play it by yourself! To begin with, DO NOT look at the story on the page below. Fill in the blanks on this page with the words called for. Then, using the words you have selected, fill in the blank spaces in the story.

Now you've created your own hilarious MAD LIBS® game!

LETTER TO A FRIEND BACK HOME

NAME OF PERSON IN ROOM _____

ADJECTIVE _____

PLACE_____

ADJECTIVE _____

NUMBER_____

FOOD _____

PLURAL NOUN _____

ADJECTIVE _____

VERB ENDING IN "ING" _____

PLURAL NOUN _____

LANGUAGE_____

PART OF THE BODY _____

ADJECTIVE _____

ADJECTIVE _____

FOOD (PLURAL) _____

SILLY WORD (PLURAL) _____

VERB ENDING IN "ING" _____

MAD LIBS®
LETTER TO A
FRIEND BACK HOME

Dear _____,
NAME OF PERSON IN ROOM

Well, here we are at the _____ Seaside Hotel in
ADJECTIVE

_____ . The weather is _____ and
PLACE   ADJECTIVE

the temperature is _____ degrees. Our hotel room looks out
NUMBER

onto a garden filled with _____ trees and tropical
FOOD

_____ . The natives are all _____ and spend their
PLURAL NOUN   ADJECTIVE

time _____ and riding their _____ through the
VERB ENDING IN "ING"   PLURAL NOUN

streets. Most of them only speak _____ , but I can com-
LANGUAGE

municate with them by making signs with my _____ . The
PART OF THE BODY

local food is really _____ . Mostly they eat _____
ADJECTIVE   ADJECTIVE

burritos and refried _____ . Our hotel only costs a
FOOD (PLURAL)

hundred _____ a day. We are going to spend the week
SILLY WORD (PLURAL)

_____ and then come home. Wish you were here.
VERB ENDING IN "ING"

MAD LIBS® is fun to play with friends, but you can also play it by yourself! To begin with, DO NOT look at the story on the page below. Fill in the blanks on this page with the words called for. Then, using the words you have selected, fill in the blank spaces in the story.

Now you've created your own hilarious MAD LIBS® game!

VACATIONS

ADJECTIVE _____

ADJECTIVE _____

NOUN _____

NOUN _____

ANIMAL (PLURAL) _____

GAME _____

PLURAL NOUN _____

VERB ENDING IN "ING" _____

VERB ENDING IN "ING" _____

FOOD (PLURAL) _____

VERB ENDING IN "ING" _____

NOUN _____

PLANT _____

PART OF THE BODY _____

PLACE _____

VERB ENDING IN "ING" _____

ADJECTIVE _____

NUMBER _____

PLURAL NOUN _____

MAD LIBS®
VACATIONS

A vacation is when you take a trip to some _____ place
ADJECTIVE

with your _____ family. Usually you go to some place that
ADJECTIVE

is near a/an _____ or up on a/an _____ . A
NOUN   NOUN

good vacation place is one where you can ride _____ or
ANIMAL (PLURAL)

play _____ or go hunting for _____ . I like
GAME   PLURAL NOUN

to spend my time _____ or _____ .
VERB ENDING IN "ING"   VERB ENDING IN "ING"

When parents go on a vacation, they spend their time eating three

_____ a day, and fathers play golf, and mothers sit around
FOOD (PLURAL)

_____ . Last summer, my little brother fell in a/an
VERB ENDING IN "ING"

_____ and got poison _____ all over his
NOUN   PLANT

_____ . My family is going to go to _____ ,
PART OF THE BODY   PLACE

and I will practice _____ . Parents need vacations
VERB ENDING IN "ING"

more than kids because parents are always very _____
ADJECTIVE

and because they have to work _____ hours every day all year
NUMBER

making enough _____ to pay for the vacation.
PLURAL NOUN

From VACATION FUN MAD LIBS® • Copyright © 1988 by Price Stern Sloan,
a division of Penguin Putnam Books for Young Readers, New York.

MAD LIBS® is fun to play with friends, but you can also play it by yourself! To begin with, DO NOT look at the story on the page below. Fill in the blanks on this page with the words called for. Then, using the words you have selected, fill in the blank spaces in the story.

Now you've created your own hilarious MAD LIBS® game!

COMPUTER CAMP

PLURAL NOUN _____

VERB _____

FOREIGN COUNTRY _____

PLURAL NOUN _____

ADJECTIVE_____

PLURAL NOUN _____

ADJECTIVE_____

NOUN _____

PUBLIC EVENT _____

NOUN _____

NOUN _____

PLURAL NOUN _____

NOUN _____

MAD LIBS®
COMPUTER CAMP

Last year I took my vacation at a computer camp. There were forty-

two _____ there, and we spent four hours every morning
　　　　　PLURAL NOUN

learning how to _____ on the computer. Computers can
　　　　　　　　　　VERB

give you instant access to information such as how many adult males

in _____ are married to _____ . Or
　　FOREIGN COUNTRY　　　　　　　　　　　PLURAL NOUN

which U.S. President passed the _____ bill regulating
　　　　　　　　　　　　　　　　　ADJECTIVE

_____ . You can also get _____ discs that will
　PLURAL NOUN　　　　　　　　　　ADJECTIVE

let you play electronic games using your computer's _____ ,
　　　　　　　　　　　　　　　　　　　　　　　NOUN

and computers can project coming events and tell you when the next

_____ will be held. And what the gross national
　PUBLIC EVENT

_____ was in 1999. A computer can also be used as a/an
　NOUN

_____ processor. It will print letters or business reports
　NOUN

or _____ . It was very educational, but this year I am
　　PLURAL NOUN

going to a/an _____ camp.
　　　　　　　NOUN

From VACATION FUN MAD LIBS® • Copyright © 1988 by Price Stern Sloan,
a division of Penguin Putnam Books for Young Readers, New York.

MAD LIBS® is fun to play with friends, but you can also play it by yourself! To begin with, DO NOT look at the story on the page below. Fill in the blanks on this page with the words called for. Then, using the words you have selected, fill in the blank spaces in the story.

Now you've created your own hilarious MAD LIBS® game!

GHOST STORY

ADJECTIVE_____

ADJECTIVE_____

PLACE _____

ANIMAL (PLURAL) _____

VERB ENDING IN "ING" _____

PLURAL NOUN _____

ADJECTIVE_____

NAME OF PERSON IN ROOM_____

PLURAL NOUN _____

NOUN _____

PLURAL NOUN _____

PLURAL NOUN _____

ADVERB_____

LAST NAME OF PERSON (PLURAL) _____

NOUN _____

SILLY NOISE _____

SILLY NOISE _____

MAD LIBS®
GHOST STORY

Once there was a little kid who went on a/an _____
ADJECTIVE

hike through a/an _____ forest in the middle of
ADJECTIVE

_____. At first he had fun watching the cute little
PLACE

_____ go _____ through the trees and
ANIMAL (PLURAL)   VERB ENDING IN "ING"

talking to the _____ that dodged between the bushes.
PLURAL NOUN

Then it began to get _____. Soon it was night, and this
ADJECTIVE

kid whose name was _____ realized he was lost,
NAME OF PERSON IN ROOM

and he got very frightened. His _____ began to chatter
PLURAL NOUN

and he wished he were home with his daddy and _____.
NOUN

Suddenly he noted that the huge trees began to look like _____,
PLURAL NOUN

and they seemed to reach out their _____ to grab him. Then
PLURAL NOUN

he saw a weird shape floating in the air and glowing _____.
ADVERB

It made a scary noise and said, "I am the spirit of the last of the

_____. I am lonely haunting this forest alone,
LAST NAME OF PERSON (PLURAL)

and I came to find some _____ to help me." Then it went
NOUN

_____ and the kid said, "_____," and that was
SILLY NOISE   SILLY NOISE

the last anyone ever heard of him. Boo!

From VACATION FUN MAD LIBS® • Copyright © 1988 by Price Stern Sloan,
a division of Penguin Putnam Books for Young Readers, New York.

MAD LIBS® is fun to play with friends, but you can also play it by yourself! To begin with, DO NOT look at the story on the page below. Fill in the blanks on this page with the words called for. Then, using the words you have selected, fill in the blank spaces in the story.

Now you've created your own hilarious MAD LIBS® game!

DRIVING IN THE CAR

PLACE _____

YEAR _____

NUMBER _____

ADJECTIVE _____

VERB ENDING IN "ING" _____

VERB ENDING IN "ING" _____

PLURAL NOUN _____

NOUN _____

NAME OF PERSON _____

ADJECTIVE _____

NOUN _____

NOUN _____

VERB ENDING IN "ING" _____

NUMBER _____

VERB _____

NOUN _____

SAME NOUN _____

VERB ENDING IN "ING" _____

ADVERB _____

ADJECTIVE _____

MAD LIBS®
DRIVING IN THE CAR

Last summer on our vacation, my father drove us to _____.
                                                          PLACE

Our car is a/an _____ sedan with _____ doors and
                     YEAR   NUMBER

a/an _____ motor. We started out at sunrise. My mother
        ADJECTIVE

and father spent all night _____ the house and
                              VERB ENDING IN "ING"

_____ the car so we could get an early start.
VERB ENDING IN "ING"

My father took his golf _____ and my mother took her
                              PLURAL NOUN

tennis _____. I took my dog, _____. The
           NOUN   NAME OF PERSON

dog and I and my little _____ sister sat in the back. My
                              ADJECTIVE

father was the driver, and as he came out of the driveway he ran into

a/an _____ and dented a/an _____. My
          NOUN   NOUN

mother said, "Why don't you pay attention and watch where you are

_____?" After _____ hours, we stopped to
VERB ENDING IN "ING"   NUMBER

_____ at a _____. The _____ was
     VERB   NOUN   SAME NOUN

horrible, and this got my father _____ again. After
                                    VERB ENDING IN "ING"

driving _____ in this manner for two days, we finally
              ADVERB

arrived here and have been having a really _____ time.
                                                 ADJECTIVE

MAD LIBS® is fun to play with friends, but you can also play it by yourself! To begin with, DO NOT look at the story on the page below. Fill in the blanks on this page with the words called for. Then, using the words you have selected, fill in the blank spaces in the story.

Now you've created your own hilarious MAD LIBS® game!

THE BAKERY

ADJECTIVE _____

NOUN _____

SOMETHING ROUND (PLURAL) _____

PLURAL NOUN _____

FLAVOR _____

NUMBER _____

FOOD (PLURAL) _____

FLAVOR _____

NUMBER _____

PLURAL NOUN _____

NUMBER _____

PLURAL NOUN _____

COLOR _____

NOUN _____

MAD LIBS®
THE BAKERY

CLERK: Good day, Miss. What can I do for you?

CUSTOMER: I want to buy some _____ bread.
                                                    ADJECTIVE

CLERK: Do you want a loaf of whole-grain _____ or would
                                                                    NOUN

              you like some buttermilk _____?
                                              SOMETHING ROUND (PLURAL)

CUSTOMER: Just a regular loaf with sesame _____ on it.
                                                          PLURAL NOUN

CLERK: All right now, how about some nice _____ cake?
                                                              FLAVOR

CUSTOMER: Well, I have _____ children, and they all like to eat
                              NUMBER

              sweet _____. How much are your cookies?
                        FOOD (PLURAL)

CLERK: We have _____ chip cookies at _____
                              FLAVOR   NUMBER

              dollars a pound. And we have this box of assorted little

              _____ for only two dollars.
                      PLURAL NOUN

CUSTOMER: I'll take one. They look like they don't have more than

              _____ calories.
                  NUMBER

CLERK: All right. That will be one box of _____, our
                                                      PLURAL NOUN

              special _____ berry pie, and a big family-sized
                          COLOR

              loaf of _____.
                          NOUN

From VACATION FUN MAD LIBS® • Copyright © 1988 by Price Stern Sloan,
a division of Penguin Putnam Books for Young Readers, New York.

MAD LIBS® is fun to play with friends, but you can also play it by yourself! To begin with, DO NOT look at the story on the page below. Fill in the blanks on this page with the words called for. Then, using the words you have selected, fill in the blank spaces in the story.

Now you've created your own hilarious MAD LIBS® game!

THE TOY STORE

SILLY WORD _____

ADJECTIVE _____

NOUN _____

PLURAL NOUN _____

PLURAL NOUN _____

ADJECTIVE _____

PLURAL NOUN _____

NUMBER _____

ADJECTIVE _____

NOUN _____

ADVERB _____

ADJECTIVE _____

ADJECTIVE _____

PERSON IN ROOM (MALE) _____

NOUN _____

MAD LIBS®
THE TOY STORE

CLERK: Good day. Welcome to the _____ Toy

                                     SILLY WORD

                   Shop. What can I do for you?

CUSTOMER: I would like to get a/an _____ toy for my

                                    ADJECTIVE

                   little _____ .

                           NOUN

CLERK: Would you like some colored _____? They

                                    PLURAL NOUN

                   stick together so you child can make _____

                                               PLURAL NOUN

                   out of them.

CUSTOMER: No, my son eats anything that is _____ .

                                        ADJECTIVE

CLERK: Here are some stuffed _____ . They are very

                                    PLURAL NOUN

                   popular with _____-year-olds.

                             NUMBER

CUSTOMER: My son is a very _____ child. Last Christmas

                                 ADJECTIVE

                   he broke the _____ we gave him.

                                 NOUN

CLERK: It is important that toys can be used _____ .

                                              ADVERB

                   For instance, this combination walkie-talkie and rubber-

                   ducky meets the _____ and _____

                                 ADJECTIVE   ADJECTIVE

                   needs of children.

CUSTOMER: That's very nice, but I am sure little _____

                                       PERSON IN ROOM (MALE)

                   would get bored with it after a few conversations in the

                   tub. I think I'll get him a/an _____ , as long

                                           NOUN

                   as it is unbreakable.

MAD LIBS® is fun to play with friends, but you can also play it by yourself! To begin with, DO NOT look at the story on the page below. Fill in the blanks on this page with the words called for. Then, using the words you have selected, fill in the blank spaces in the story.

Now you've created your own hilarious MAD LIBS® game!

VACATION SPORTS

ADJECTIVE _____

NUMBER _____

PLURAL NOUN _____

ANIMAL _____

SPORT _____

VERB ENDING IN "ING" _____

ADJECTIVE _____

VERB ENDING IN "ING" _____

VERB ENDING IN "ING" _____

NUMBER _____

PLURAL NOUN _____

NUMBER _____

NOUN _____

NOUN _____

NOUN _____

ADVERB _____

MAD LIBS®
VACATION SPORTS

There are many new and _____ things you can do on your
                              ADJECTIVE

vacation today. _____ years ago, _____ who went
                    NUMBER   PLURAL NOUN

on a vacation could play tennis or go _____ -back riding,
                                              ANIMAL

or play 18 holes of _____ , or spend their time
                              SPORT

_____ with their family. But today, if you are
   VERB ENDING IN "ING"

_____ enough to try, you can go skydiving, or wind surfing,
   ADJECTIVE

or water skiing, or mountain _____. Skydiving is the
                                    VERB ENDING IN "ING"

most fun, if you are not afraid of _____. First, you
                                        VERB ENDING IN "ING"

strap on _____ parachutes. Then you get in an airplane with
             NUMBER

eight or nine other _____ and go up to _____
                          PLURAL NOUN   NUMBER

feet. Then you open the door and jump out. Once in the air, everyone

holds hands and you go into a free fall towards the _____
                                                          NOUN

below. At the last minute, you yank on your _____ and open
                                                  NOUN

your parachute and float gently to the _____. It is a lot of
                                              NOUN

fun if you like to live _____.
                              ADVERB

MAD LIBS® is fun to play with friends, but you can also play it by yourself! To begin with, DO NOT look at the story on the page below. Fill in the blanks on this page with the words called for. Then, using the words you have selected, fill in the blank spaces in the story.

Now you've created your own hilarious MAD LIBS® game!

THE HIGH SCHOOL MONSTER

ADJECTIVE _____

TOWN _____

ADJECTIVE _____

PERSON IN ROOM (FEMALE) _____

PERSON IN ROOM (MALE) _____

PLURAL NOUN _____

VERB (PAST TENSE) _____

PET NAME _____

NOUN _____

NAME OF PERSON _____

NUMBER _____

ADJECTIVE _____

COLOR _____

PERSON IN ROOM _____

ADJECTIVE _____

ADJECTIVE _____

ADVERB _____

NOUN _____

MAD LIBS®
THE HIGH SCHOOL MONSTER

NARRATOR: Our scene is in a/an _____ high school in
ADJECTIVE

_____ . The students are _____ with
TOWN   ADJECTIVE

fear. Listen as our heroine, _____ ,
PERSON IN ROOM (FEMALE)

speaks to _____ .
PERSON IN ROOM (MALE)

GIRL: The High School Monster has eaten three more

pretty young _____ and _____
PLURAL NOUN   VERB (PAST TENSE)

the Chemistry teacher.

BOY: Don't be afraid, _____ . I think the monster
PET NAME

is really just a _____ .
NOUN

GIRL: But _____ saw it. It has _____
NAME OF PERSON   NUMBER

arms and long _____ hair and _____ teeth.
ADJECTIVE   COLOR

BOY: Hmm. That sounds like _____ .
PERSON IN ROOM

I am going to set a trap for this so-called monster. And

you must be the _____ bait.
ADJECTIVE

GIRL: Oh, no! Do I look _____ ? When I go
ADJECTIVE

out I walk very _____ . Get some
ADVERB

other _____ .
NOUN

From VACATION FUN MAD LIBS® • Copyright © 1988 by Price Stern Sloan,
a division of Penguin Putnam Books for Young Readers, New York.

MAD LIBS® is fun to play with friends, but you can also play it by yourself! To begin with, DO NOT look at the story on the page below. Fill in the blanks on this page with the words called for. Then, using the words you have selected, fill in the blank spaces in the story.

Now you've created your own hilarious MAD LIBS® game!

GOING ON A "DIG"

PLURAL NOUN _____

NOUN _____

PLURAL NOUN _____

VERB ENDING IN "ING" _____

ADJECTIVE _____

ONE-SYLLABLE WORD _____

NOUN _____

NUMBER _____

PART OF THE BODY _____

ADJECTIVE _____

TYPE OF FOOD _____

TYPE OF FOOD _____

TYPE OF FOOD _____

NOUN _____

PLURAL NOUN _____

ADJECTIVE _____

ADJECTIVE _____

MAD LIBS®
GOING ON A "DIG"

A "dig" is what archaeologists call it when a bunch of _____

_____
PLURAL NOUN

go to a desert and look for old bones and pieces of _____

_____
NOUN

and fossilized _____ . _____ and looking for
_____   _____
PLURAL NOUN   VERB ENDING IN "ING"

dinosaur bones is really a/an _____ way to spend a vacation.
_____
ADJECTIVE

Last year I dug up the jawbone of a tyrannosaurus _____ .
_____
ONE-SYLLABLE WORD

The tyrannosaurus is my favorite _____ . It was _____
_____   _____
NOUN   NUMBER

feet tall and had a huge _____ with hundreds of _____
_____   _____
PART OF THE BODY   ADJECTIVE

teeth. It was carnivorous and would only eat _____ . The
_____
TYPE OF FOOD

brontosaurus and diplodocus were herbivorous, which means they

would only eat _____ or sometimes, _____ . If
_____   _____
TYPE OF FOOD   TYPE OF FOOD

you go on a "dig," you might also find old pieces of _____
_____
NOUN

or ancient Indian _____ or pieces of _____
_____   _____
PLURAL NOUN   ADJECTIVE

pottery. You can sell this sort of thing to _____ museums
_____
ADJECTIVE

for enough to pay for your trip.

From VACATION FUN MAD LIBS® • Copyright © 1988 by Price Stern Sloan,
a division of Penguin Putnam Books for Young Readers, New York.

MAD LIBS® is fun to play with friends, but you can also play it by yourself! To begin with, DO NOT look at the story on the page below. Fill in the blanks on this page with the words called for. Then, using the words you have selected, fill in the blank spaces in the story.

Now you've created your own hilarious MAD LIBS® game!

VACATION WANT ADS

CITY _____

NOUN _____

ADJECTIVE_____

SCHOOL _____

VERB ENDING IN "ING" _____

FIRST NAME (FEMALE) _____

ADJECTIVE_____

ADJECTIVE_____

SOMETHING ALIVE _____

NOUN _____

VERB ENDING IN "ING" _____

ADJECTIVE_____

PLURAL NOUN _____

ANIMAL (PLURAL) _____

ADVERB_____

NOUN _____

MAD☺LIBS®
VACATION WANT ADS

DRIVER AVAILABLE. Are you planning a trip to _____?
                                              CITY

I will drive your _____. I am a person of _____
                      NOUN   ADJECTIVE

character and a graduate of _____. I have been
                                    SCHOOL

_____ for twelve years.
VERB ENDING IN "ING"

MOTHER _____ offers you _____
            FIRST NAME (FEMALE)   ADJECTIVE

accommodations in her _____ home. Only $10 per
                              ADJECTIVE

_____ for _____ and breakfast.
  SOMETHING ALIVE   NOUN

DO YOU NEED A HOUSE SITTER? While you are _____
                                              VERB ENDING IN "ING"

around the country, who is looking after your _____ house?
                                                    ADJECTIVE

Burglars could steal your _____. Who will feed your pet
                                PLURAL NOUN

_____? We will _____ take care of everything.
  ANIMAL (PLURAL)   ADVERB

Call _____ Sitters Unlimited.
          NOUN

MAD LIBS® is fun to play with friends, but you can also play it by yourself! To begin with, DO NOT look at the story on the page below. Fill in the blanks on this page with the words called for. Then, using the words you have selected, fill in the blank spaces in the story.

Now you've created your own hilarious MAD LIBS® game!

ADVERTISEMENT FOR A CRUISE SHIP

NOUN _____

NOUN _____

PLURAL NOUN _____

PLURAL NOUN _____

TYPE OF CONTAINER _____

ADJECTIVE_____

NOUN _____

PERSON IN ROOM _____

PLURAL NOUN _____

ADJECTIVE_____

CITY _____

PLACE _____

NOUN _____

CITY _____

VERB ENDING IN "ING" _____

ADVERB_____

PLURAL NOUN _____

MAD LIBS®
ADVERTISEMENT FOR A CRUISE SHIP

Come aboard the famous cruise ship, "Love _____."
NOUN

Your vacation will stretch from the land of the midnight _____
NOUN

to the sunny _____ of the Mediterranean. You and your
PLURAL NOUN

_____ will stay in a luxurious private _____.
PLURAL NOUN   TYPE OF CONTAINER

You will dine in _____ surroundings in our magnificent
ADJECTIVE

banquet hall on the _____ deck. Every night there will be
NOUN

entertainment by _____ and his/her musical
PERSON IN ROOM

_____. The _____ cruise will visit the
PLURAL NOUN   ADJECTIVE

island port of _____ and then go along the coast
CITY

of _____. We will drop _____ in
PLACE   NOUN

_____ and spend all day _____. You can live
CITY   VERB ENDING IN "ING"

_____ and all for only 120 _____ a day, plus tax.
ADVERB   PLURAL NOUN

MAD LIBS® is fun to play with friends, but you can also play it by yourself! To begin with, DO NOT look at the story on the page below. Fill in the blanks on this page with the words called for. Then, using the words you have selected, fill in the blank spaces in the story.

Now you've created your own hilarious MAD LIBS® game!

DIALOGUE BETWEEN TOURIST AND SALESPERSON

PERSON IN ROOM (MALE)_____

PERSON IN ROOM (FEMALE)_____

PLURAL NOUN _____

PLURAL NOUN _____

TOWN_____

ADJECTIVE_____

NOUN _____

PLURAL NOUN _____

ADJECTIVE_____

CITY _____

VEGETABLE_____

COLOR_____

NOUN _____

NOUN _____

NUMBER _____

ADJECTIVE_____

MAD●LIBS®
DIALOGUE BETWEEN
TOURIST AND SALESPERSON

Played by _____ *and* _____ .
PERSON IN ROOM (MALE)   PERSON IN ROOM (FEMALE)

BOY: Hello there, Miss. I am looking for some postal _____
PLURAL NOUN

that I can mail back to my _____ in _____ .
PLURAL NOUN   TOWN

GIRL: We have some very _____ cards. Would you like
ADJECTIVE

some with pictures of our local _____ or with
NOUN

pictures of _____ growing along the beach?
PLURAL NOUN

BOY: I would like five of those that show my _____ hotel.
ADJECTIVE

GIRL: All right. Now, how about this bumper sticker that says

"_____ , America's greatest little _____ "?
CITY   VEGETABLE

BOY: No thanks. But I would like to see one of those _____
COLOR

hats with the _____ on top.
NOUN

GIRL: Okay. Here. My, you look just like a _____ .
NOUN

BOY: Good. I'll take it. Now if you can sell me some _____-
NUMBER

cent stamps, I'll let all my friends back home know what a/an

_____ time I am having.
ADJECTIVE

From VACATION FUN MAD LIBS® • Copyright © 1988 by Price Stern Sloan,
a division of Penguin Putnam Books for Young Readers, New York.

MAD LIBS® is fun to play with friends, but you can also play it by yourself! To begin with, DO NOT look at the story on the page below. Fill in the blanks on this page with the words called for. Then, using the words you have selected, fill in the blank spaces in the story.

Now you've created your own hilarious MAD LIBS® game!

LETTER FROM AN AMERICAN IN PARIS

ADJECTIVE_____

PERSON IN ROOM _____

ADJECTIVE_____

ADVERB_____

PLURAL NOUN _____

LAST NAME OF PERSON _____

NOUN _____

SILLY WORD_____

LAST NAME OF PERSON _____

FIRST NAME (FEMALE) _____

ITALIAN WORD _____

NOUN _____

PLURAL NOUN _____

PLURAL NOUN _____

ADJECTIVE_____

ADJECTIVE_____

FRUIT _____

VERB _____

VERB _____

MAD LIBS®
LETTER FROM
AN AMERICAN IN PARIS

Dear _____ _____,
     ADJECTIVE   PERSON IN ROOM

I am having a/an _____ time here in Paris. I spend
         ADJECTIVE

every day _____ visiting museums, monuments, and
     ADVERB

_____. Yesterday I went to the _____
PLURAL NOUN   LAST NAME OF PERSON

Tower, which is located on the river _____. Then I
       NOUN

went to the Jeu de Pomme. This is a museum that is spelled J-E-U D-E

P-O-M-M-E and is pronounced _____. It is next to the Louvre,
      SILLY WORD

which has the famous statue of Venus de _____
            LAST NAME OF PERSON

and the painting of the Mona _____ by Leonardo
      FIRST NAME (FEMALE)

da _____. The center of Paris is called the Place of
  ITALIAN WORD

the _____ and is always filled with thousands of
    NOUN

_____ all taking photographs of each other and of the many
PLURAL NOUN

French _____. The food at the Paris restaurants is
     PLURAL NOUN

_____. I have already eaten _____ snails and
ADJECTIVE   ADJECTIVE

duck a la _____. I plan to _____ to Paris again next
    FRUIT   VERB

year and hope you can _____, too.
           VERB

From VACATION FUN MAD LIBS® • Copyright © 1988 by Price Stern Sloan,
a division of Penguin Putnam Books for Young Readers, New York.

MAD LIBS® is fun to play with friends, but you can also play it by yourself! To begin with, DO NOT look at the story on the page below. Fill in the blanks on this page with the words called for. Then, using the words you have selected, fill in the blank spaces in the story.

Now you've created your own hilarious MAD LIBS® game!

A QUIZ TO TAKE BEFORE LEAVING HOME

LIQUID _____

NOUN _____

ANIMAL _____

SAME ANIMAL _____

PART OF THE BODY _____

PART OF THE BODY _____

ADJECTIVE _____

SPORT _____

ADJECTIVE _____

ADJECTIVE _____

FOOD (PLURAL) _____

ADJECTIVE _____

COUNTRY _____

PLURAL NOUN _____

NOUN _____

NOUN _____

EXCLAMATION _____

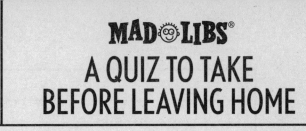

MAD LIBS®
A QUIZ TO TAKE
BEFORE LEAVING HOME

1. Have you filled your car with _____?
   _____LIQUID_____

2. Do you have the reservations for your room at the _____?
   _____NOUN

3. Are you taking your pet _____ in the car? If so, have
   _____ANIMAL

   you plenty of _____ Chow for him?
   _____SAME ANIMAL

4. Did you remember to pack all of your toilet articles, such as your

   _____ brush and your _____ paste and
   PART OF THE BODY   PART OF THE BODY

   your _____ lotion?
   _____ADJECTIVE

5. Did you bring your tennis balls, your _____ racket, and
   _____SPORT

   those _____ athletic shoes?
   _____ADJECTIVE

6. Have you got a map that shows all of the _____ roads
   _____ADJECTIVE

   and the places that serve _____ and have nice, clean
   _____FOOD (PLURAL)

   _____ rooms?
   _____ADJECTIVE

7. Did you remember to bring your _____ traveler's
   _____COUNTRY

   checks and plenty of money in small _____?
   _____PLURAL NOUN

8. Did you remember to turn off the _____ and the
   _____NOUN

   _____ in the house?
   _____NOUN

If you answered "_____!" to these questions, you can
   _____EXCLAMATION

leave at once.

From VACATION FUN MAD LIBS® • Copyright © 1988 by Price Stern Sloan,
a division of Penguin Putnam Books for Young Readers, New York.

MAD LIBS® is fun to play with friends, but you can also play it by yourself! To begin with, DO NOT look at the story on the page below. Fill in the blanks on this page with the words called for. Then, using the words you have selected, fill in the blank spaces in the story.

Now you've created your own hilarious MAD LIBS® game!

A LETTER TO A RESORT HOTEL

LAST NAME OF PERSON IN ROOM _____

NAME OF PERSON _____

TOWN _____

NOUN _____

NOUN _____

ADJECTIVE _____

PLURAL NOUN _____

NOUN _____

PLURAL NOUN _____

ADJECTIVE _____

FOOD _____

LIQUID _____

PLACE _____

LAST NAME OF PERSON _____

NOUN _____

ADJECTIVE _____

ADJECTIVE _____

ADVERB _____

NOUN _____

MAD LIBS®
A LETTER TO
A RESORT HOTEL

To the Manager of _____ 's Hotel,
LAST NAME OF PERSON IN ROOM

344 _____ Street, _____ , California.
NAME OF PERSON   TOWN

Dear Sir, Madam or _____ ,
NOUN

I would like to reserve a/an _____ at your _____
NOUN   ADJECTIVE

hotel for two weeks in August. We will need a room for myself, my

wife, and our two _____ . We would like a double
PLURAL NOUN

_____ with a view of the _____ . I understand
NOUN   PLURAL NOUN

that your rate includes a continental breakfast consisting of a/an

_____ French roll and _____ preserves and a pot
ADJECTIVE   FOOD

of hot _____ . I would also like to reserve a side trip to
LIQUID

_____ and to the _____ Canyon. My wife and
PLACE   LAST NAME OF PERSON

I will go to the canyon alone. We will leave our smallest _____
NOUN

with his _____ brother at the swimming pool. We were at
ADJECTIVE

your hotel last year and had a simply _____ time, and we
ADJECTIVE

look forward to fourteen days of relaxing _____ in your
ADVERB

luxurious _____ .
NOUN

From VACATION FUN MAD LIBS® • Copyright © 1988 by Price Stern Sloan,
a division of Penguin Putnam Books for Young Readers, New York.

MAD LIBS® is fun to play with friends, but you can also play it by yourself! To begin with, DO NOT look at the story on the page below. Fill in the blanks on this page with the words called for. Then, using the words you have selected, fill in the blank spaces in the story.

Now you've created your own hilarious MAD LIBS® game!

HOW TO ENJOY YOURSELF ON THE BEACH

TYPE OF LIQUID _____

SOMETHING ICKY _____

PIECE OF FURNITURE (PLURAL) _____

ARTICLE OF CLOTHING_____

COLOR_____

PART OF THE BODY _____

PLURAL NOUN _____

ADJECTIVE_____

ADJECTIVE_____

PLURAL NOUN _____

ANIMAL _____

SILLY WORD_____

ADJECTIVE_____

ADVERB_____

MAD LIBS®
HOW TO ENJOY YOURSELF ON THE BEACH

When you go to the beach, you must take along a big blanket, a

thermos bottle full of _____ , lots of suntan
TYPE OF LIQUID

_____ , and a couple of folding _____ .
SOMETHING ICKY PIECE OF FURNITURE (PLURAL)

Then you put on your _____ so you can get a beautiful
ARTICLE OF CLOTHING

_____ to last you all summer. You also should have a big
COLOR

hat to keep the sun off your _____ . If you want
PART OF THE BODY

exercise, you can find some _____ to play volleyball with.
PLURAL NOUN

Volleyball is America's favorite _____ game. You can also
ADJECTIVE

bring a/an _____ lunch, such as hard-boiled _____ ,
ADJECTIVE PLURAL NOUN

a few _____ sandwiches with mustard, and some bottles
ANIMAL

of _____ cola. If you remember all of the above and get
SILLY WORD

a place near a/an _____ lifeguard, you can sunbathe
ADJECTIVE

_____ all day.
ADVERB

From VACATION FUN MAD LIBS® • Copyright © 1988 by Price Stern Sloan,
a division of Penguin Putnam Books for Young Readers, New York.

MAD LIBS® is fun to play with friends, but you can also play it by yourself! To begin with, DO NOT look at the story on the page below. Fill in the blanks on this page with the words called for. Then, using the words you have selected, fill in the blank spaces in the story.

Now you've created your own hilarious MAD LIBS® game!

REVIEWS OF ENTERTAINERS APPEARING AT RESORTS

FIRST NAME (MALE)_____

FIRST NAME (FEMALE)_____

ADJECTIVE _____

NOUN _____

PLURAL NOUN_____

ADJECTIVE _____

PLACE_____

PERSON IN ROOM (MALE) _____

SILLY WORD _____

SAME SILLY WORD_____

PLURAL NOUN_____

ADJECTIVE _____

ADJECTIVE _____

ARTICLE OF CLOTHING _____

NOUN _____

PERSON IN ROOM _____

PERSON IN ROOM _____

PERSON IN ROOM _____

ADJECTIVE _____

VERB _____

VERB _____

NUMBER_____

POPULAR ROCK STAR _____

MAD LIBS®
REVIEWS OF ENTERTAINERS
APPEARING IN RESORTS

_____ and _____ made their debut
   FIRST NAME (MALE)   FIRST NAME (FEMALE)

as a really _____ singing act at the _____
           ADJECTIVE   NOUN

Lounge. The songs they sang ranged from a series of crowd-pleasing

old _____ to _____ songs from England, Spain,
    PLURAL NOUN   ADJECTIVE

and _____ . Good summer entertainment.
        PLACE

A young comedian named _____ opened at the
                  PERSON IN ROOM (MALE)

_____ Room of the _____ Hotel last night.
  SILLY WORD   SAME SILLY WORD

He began with a monologue of one-line _____ , which
                         PLURAL NOUN

garnered _____ laughter from the audience. Then he
        ADJECTIVE

donned a/an _____ comical _____ and
           ADJECTIVE   ARTICLE OF CLOTHING

performed a pantomime of a customer in a pet store trying to buy

a/an _____ . This should be a good bet for television.
     NOUN

_____ and _____ , the dancing twins,
  PERSON IN ROOM   PERSON IN ROOM

headline the _____ Hotel with their _____
        PERSON IN ROOM   ADJECTIVE

act. The twins present their version of the _____ and also
                           VERB

do their interpretation of the _____ . For the grand finale,
                   VERB

the duo does a _____-step to the music of _____ .
        NUMBER   POPULAR ROCK STAR